Sharing
GOD'S LOVE
with Others

Sharing GOD'S LOVE with Others

Written by Mary Moore Wyatt

Illustrated by Ted Bolte

Publishing House
St. Louis

With love and thanks to God
and to my family

(And Jesus said to His followers,) "Go therefore and make
disciples of all nations, baptizing them in the name of the
Father, and of the Son, and of the Holy Spirit, teaching them
to observe all that I have commanded you; and lo, I am with
you always to the close of the age." Matthew 28:19-20

Library of Congress Catalog Card Number:
ISBN 0-570-07795-8
Printed in the United States of America

God's love is wonderful!
Share it with someone today!

God's love is like a gift.
He gave us His Son Jesus.
Tell someone about Jesus today.

God's love is like a window.
Through it you can see the sunshine.
Say something nice to someone today.

God's love is like a leap.
It brings joy.
    Tell someone about your joy today.

God's love is like a flower.
It is beautiful.
　　Surprise someone this very day.

God's love is like a tree.
It watches over you.
Plant a seed of friendship and watch it grow.

God's love is like a mountain.
It is strong.
Make peace with an enemy today.

God's love is like a lamb.
It is gentle.
Help someone who is in need.

God's love is like a smile.
It tells you that you are loved.
Smile at someone right now.
(Wait and see, they may smile back.)

God's love is like a special treat.
It makes you feel good through and through.
Remember someone far away.

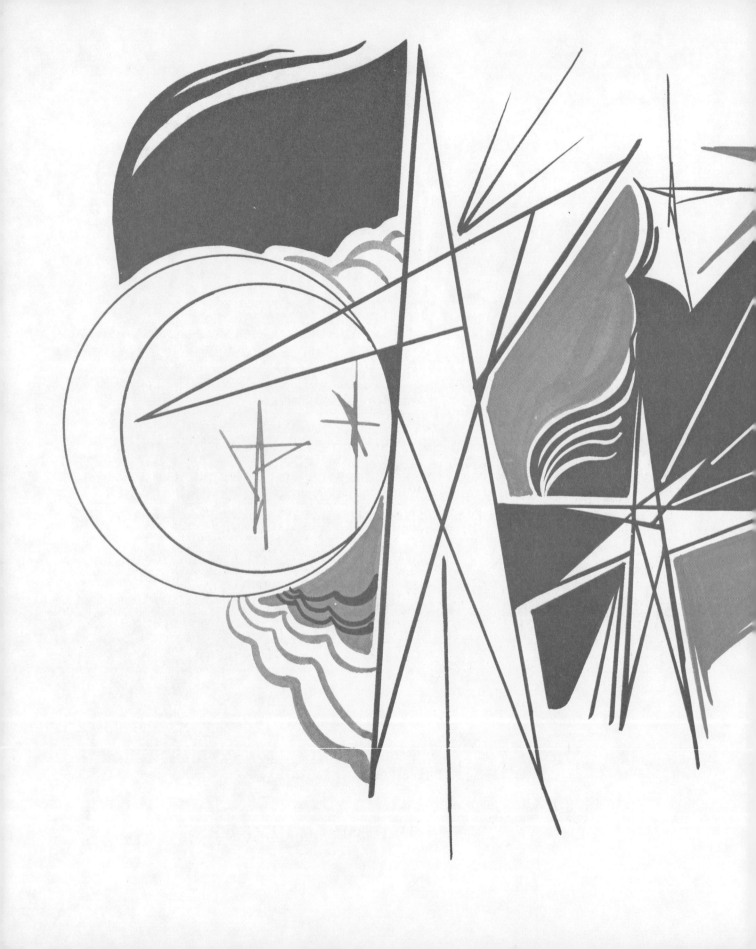

God's love is like a star.
It shines.
    Did you make someone happy today?

Dear Parents:

A young 14-year-old boy once said to his teacher: "The hardest part of being a Christian is admitting to others I am one." How tragic for all of us! What if the disciples and the early Christians had kept the Good News to themselves. But how could they! For Jesus says, "You are the light of the world. A city set on a hill cannot be hid. Nor do men light a lamp and put it under a bushel, but on a stand, and it gives light to all in the house. Let your light so shine before men that they may see your good works and give glory to your Father who is in Heaven" (Matthew 5:14-16).

Over and over again we read in Holy Scripture that God's steadfast love endures forever. And because God loves us He sent His Son to die for us in our stead (John 3:16). Out of love for Him we try to live as he wants us to live; loving our neighbors— including our enemies—and serving them, and spreading the Good News to others. See Christ's words of the Great Commission in the front of this book.

It is part of our Christian responsibility to share God's love and the Gospel message. Teach your children at an early age by word and example to share this wonderful message with others.

The Editor